Wow!

Adding Pizzazz to Teaching and Learning

Also by Stephen G. Barkley:

Quality Teaching in a Culture of Coaching

Adding Pizzazz to Teaching and Learning

By Stephen G. Barkley

with Contributing Editor Terri Bianco

PERFORMANCE
LEARNING SYSTEMS.

Performance Learning Systems, Inc.®

Performance Learning Systems, Inc.® Publications Division
© 2005 Performance Learning Systems, Inc.
All Rights Reserved.
Printed in the United States of America
10 9 8 7 6 5 4 3 2 1

PLS® Products
72 Lone Oak Drive
Cadiz, KY 42211
800-506-9996
Fax 270-522-2014
http://www.plsweb.com/resources/products/books/wow/

Library of Congress Cataloging-to-Publication Data

Barkley, Stephen G. (Stephen George), 1950-
  Wow! : adding pizzazz to teaching and learning / Stephen G. Barkley ;
Terri Bianco, contributing editor.
     p. cm.
  Includes bibliographical references and index.
  ISBN-13: 978-1-892334-22-0 (pbk. : alk. paper)
  1. Education–United States. 2. Teaching–United States. 3.
Motivation in education–United States. I. Bianco, Terri. II. Title.
  LB14.7.B352 2005
  371.1102–dc22
                              2005025309

Cover Design & Internal Design:
Shari A. Resinger, Art Director; Sylvia Filaccio
Index: Brackney Indexing Service
Adobe Fonts: ITC Cheltenham and Berthold City

This book may be ordered from Performance Learning Systems®,
72 Lone Oak Dr., Cadiz, KY 42211, 800-506-9996.

Quantity discounts are available for bulk purchases, sales
promotions, premiums, fund-raising, and educational needs.

Dedication

This book is dedicated to
Dr. Brenda Stallion Barkley.
Brenda was the first person to respond
with excitement when I shared my thoughts
about how wonderful it would be if
the opening day of school created
a WOW! reaction from students.
She immediately expanded and
implemented WOWs into her teaching.
As my wife and friend, she continually
amazes and WOWs me.

Contents

Acknowledgments

A special acknowledgment goes to Beth Provancha, an outstanding Florida educator whose WOW is cited in Chapter Three. Beth's untimely death was a loss to many colleagues, parents, and students who were grateful recipients of her caring and lively WOWs.

I would like to express my sincere appreciation and admiration to the team that helped develop this book and to all the educators throughout this country who have designed and developed rich, creative, and useful learning tools.

The following teachers and administrators have added the concept of WOW to their toolboxes and have shared some of them with us. I greatly appreciate and acknowledge Freda Abercrombie, Ruth Angert, Neil Bress, Pat Carroll, Richard Ellenburg, Peggy Hollis, Kevin Kendrick, Dr. Jean Linder, Bruce Malnor, Steve Mintner, Barbie Pagano, Steve Sassaman,

Andrea Schmidt, Dr. Brenda Stallion, Joe Sullivan, Mark Thompson, Kathy Weiland, and Cheryl Wood.

My thanks to Terri Bianco, TB Enterprises, for her enthusiasm, support, and terrific writing and editing skills. Barbara Brown at Performance Learning Systems® for her editing and efficiency in shepherding the manuscript through the layout and printing process. Kit Bailey of Second Look Proofreading and Editing. Shari Resinger and Sylvia Filaccio, Victor Printing, for layout and cover. Michael Brackney for his index.

Introduction

In 1994 Tom Peters published *The Pursuit of WOW!*, a book aimed at helping business improve innovation in what he calls "topsy turvy" times. He describes various products and services he felt achieved exceptional customer satisfaction.

He noted companies that provided service that went above and beyond the norm. He cited examples such as how Southwest Airlines defined itself in the marketplace as a personality seeking to amuse, surprise, and entertain its passengers. How General Motors took relationship marketing to new levels when it threw a "homecoming hoedown" for its 30,000 customers who bought Saturns. How the

University Bank & Trust of Palo Alto, CA, offered customers free shoeshines, balloons for their children, and a huge bag of Walla Walla onions every August.

Flying around the country, Peters discovered examples of quality that met his growing criteria for WOW: an accounting in Ellen Langer's book *Mindfulness* about nursing home residents given house plants to care for; Odwalla fruit drinks with the bottoms of the bottles imprinted with "enjoy by ____" instead of "expires on ____"; and Ben Cohen's ice cream campaign asking customers to send in a lid from their favorite ice cream container along with a short essay on why the customer would make a good CEO of Ben & Jerry's Ice Cream®.

Peters simplified this customer satisfaction rating by noticing the product or service typically elicited the equivalent of a "wow" from customers, whether spoken in amazement, such as "**WOW!!!**" or subtly, spoken softly in awe or with the tone of having been touched, as in *"wow."*

I began to look for WOWs I happened upon. Entering a chain restaurant one evening, I was greeted by two people assigned to open the door and, as I approached, they smiled and said, "Welcome!" From this experience, I envisioned greeters at a middle school as students approached the door. When I checked into my hotel very late one night, I was handed two hot chocolate chip cookies. WOW! I wondered if kids ever feel as good as I did just then while they're at school.

Alas, it occurred to me as I flew around the country to various school sites that there was a growing dearth of WOW experiences in schools. And by WOW, Peters and I both mean many things, chief among them quality — where is there a quality experience, a quality product in schools? What do educators do to elicit a WOW from students? How could we put more of a WOW in their learning? Where were the WOW schools?

As an educator, I know students learn when there is something relevant and meaningful to them — something that hooks them and sparks their interest to pay attention to what's next. I began looking for first-day-of-school experiences as an opportunity to pique students' interest so they would be eager to come back and spend the year there.

What I found disappointed. Most first-day-of-school events consist of someone reading the rules. Someone outlines what students may and may not do. Or they may express the *hope* that students would have a good year.

I was invited to a high school on its opening day. The students came directly from the buses into a large auditorium. There the principal welcomed them and announced there were seven new regulations he intended to go over. He asked that they bear with him, as he wanted to cover each and every one. Trust me, there wasn't a "wow" uttered in that auditorium that first day of school.

I began weaving the concept of WOW into presentations I gave related to quality or to coaching programs or to learning styles — wherever I thought it would fit, but mostly in terms of quality in education. I challenged teachers to come up with first-day WOWs and let me know how they went.

Wow! The unleashed creativity of teachers and principals resulted in first-day-of-school experiences that were lively, fun, meaningful, and designed to completely WOW the students coming into school. They worked. Students were wowed. Parents heard about them from students returning home. Not just kindergarten students mentioned the wows — they are easy to WOW — but elementary, middle school, and high school students did as well.

WOW began taking on a life of its own in some schools and even within whole districts. The WOW experience became contagious. Some schools created a tradition of first-day WOWs, a tradition that is continuing today. Others expanded the WOW concept to lesson plans, parent-teacher nights, faculty meetings, and staff appreciation.

The WOW concept resonated with educators who used it. Many found WOWs not only engaged students, they created teamwork among staff and released stress that often accompanies not only the first day of school, but teaching throughout the school year.

And of course we know the research on learning soundly supports a brain-compatible environment where learning is relevant. Where there is meaning, there is learning. Learning that is multisensory, has emotion, novelty, fun, and works the way the brain works. WOWs meet brain-based criteria to a T.

This book is meant to capture many of the original and creative ideas teachers developed to create WOW learning, WOW first days of school, WOW beginnings of new subjects or projects, or WOW new anythings in school.

Some WOWs were submitted to us through interviews with teachers, others were learned from principals and administrators. Many were related to me in passing as I rode on elevators from conferences or dashed down the hallway of a school building on my way to catch a plane. Others arrived via email from teachers I never met.

All found their way into this book, whose intent is to impart the WOW concept to you in ways that will engage and motivate you to create your own WOW experiences for others.

You will learn how WOW experiences segue beautifully into meaningful learning and how brain research corroborates the value of a WOW experience. This book is not about asking teachers to entertain students with WOWs. Rather, it shows ways that adding a WOW experience can generate learning in a way that is novel, exciting, and motivating. I am confident there are as many more WOWs out there as there are creative teachers and administrators to invent them.

WOWs are meant to be fun. They are meant to engage the learner, to energize the creativity of teachers, and to give parents a sense that THIS is the school for THEIR kid because it's, well, you know, WOW!!!

Enjoy the experience. I hope that at the end you will, in fact, be sufficiently wowed to take the ideas into your classroom, your school, your teaching, and your life — because you deserve a WOW today.

WOW 101

Follow the Yellow Brick Road

It's open house at an elementary school. The teachers, principal, and staff are anticipating the arrival of the students and their parents to "greet the teacher" and welcome them to the school year that begins the following day.

Cars begin to arrive and vie for parking places in the lot. Parents usher their children out of the car and manage to juggle all the accoutrements that usually go with elementary children — drawings, bunnies, things they just *had* to bring with them to the open house. As the parents take their children's hands and walk toward the school building, they sense something is different. Music is being played somewhere, people are singing.

Curious and amused, the parents pick up the pace and move their kids along to the entrance of the building. As they walk, they find a long yellow brick road fabricated on the walkway from parking lot to school entrance. On either side of the yellow brick road are teachers, staff, custodians, the principal, and the assistant principal smiling and singing along with a loudspeaker that is blaring, *"Ease on down, ease on down, ease on down the roh-oad . . ."* from *The Wiz*, the musical based on *The Wizard of Oz*. They are clapping, greeting, and welcoming students and parents. It feels festive, exciting.

The students are confused at first, taken aback. Then they begin to smile and giggle, squeezing their parents' hands. Parents are smiling too. They feel welcomed and sense warmth. It seems their children are going to a place that is safe. Their kids will have fun and will be cared for. That's a WOW!

What if The Hokey Pokey Really IS What it's All About?

The introduction to a child development class for high school students in Clearview, NJ, consists of gathering in the main hall during lunch and being led by the teacher in performing The Hokey Pokey. Other students peek into the hall to see what the laughter is about. Later the students are showing others how to hopscotch or play with hackysacks. What better way to learn about children than to play like them?

Stop, Look, Listen, and Chew?

Students spill into their first middle school science class, chatting and bumping each other. They take their seats and look up at their teacher who is seated at her desk behind three ivory-colored candles. They're kind of pretty, but what are they *doing* there, the students wonder.

The teacher introduces herself and says they are going to have a wonderful time discovering the world of science during the coming school year. Without further ado, she lights the wicks of all three candles and asks students to take out the notepad under their desks.

She asks them to observe the candles from where they are seated, taking notes as they observe. She tells them to stop, look, listen, and write down everything they see. Prompting them, she asks what colors they see. She tells them to notice where the smoke is going, what odors they smell, and the performance of the candles — are they flickering, smoldering, or burning calmly and straight? Do they move with the movement of the students as they pass by? How? Write down everything you discover, she tells them.

As they are finished observing the scientific experiment, she blows the candles out, one by one, and asks them to write what they see and smell and notice.

As they watch and take notes, the teacher picks up the middle candle and takes a bite out of it. She chews it slowly and then eats the rest of the candle. The students drop their jaws, stupefied.

She continues to ask the students to write down what they see, what they notice and observe. As the class comes to an end, she suggests they take their observations of this first day of science class home to their parents and share what they saw, what they observed, what they learned. Because, she said, this is what science is all about.

With that, she dismissed the class.

As it turns out, the middle candle was carved out of a potato, ivory in color, and an oily almond sliver was used as a wick. It was a well-camouflaged candle. Not noticing that because of their perception, however, students were completely intrigued and curious about what happened in that science class.

They went home excited, telling their parents about the teacher who ate the candle. They couldn't wait to come back to discover what it was all about, *discover* being the operative word the science teacher was after. This not only excited the students; the parents were also intrigued.

Hats Off to Gardening!

At Kemp Elementary School in Cobb County, GA, parents drop their children off and quickly grab the home video camera to record their child walking into school on his or her first day. To their surprise, teachers throughout the school are wearing flowerpot hats on their heads. Each teacher sports a different chapeau that resembles a tumbling array of petunias or sunflowers or basil. Some are dressed in gardening clothes. Others are in a costume resembling the greenery of the plant they have become. Excitement soars. Teachers are smiling, repeating WOW at every pass: "Wow, did you see that?" "Wow, how wonderful you look!" "Wow! This is going to be a year of FUN!" Parents get caught up in the excitement, videotaping their children's reactions, each teacher's garb, capturing the whole scene.

Wow.

WOW Signals Quality

What is this thing called "wow"? It can be many things and take on many forms. The most important aspect of the WOW concept lies in its focus on gaining the positive attention of students — or teachers or staff or parents or other educators — that leads to learning and to action.

An element of surprise, novelty, and fun is present in any WOW experience. There is enjoyment, excitement — something's happening here. Most importantly, WOW signals quality. We recognize quality when it occurs and yet its definition is elusive, as author William Glasser, M.D., declares in this description of quality that I have always found provocative:

> *While quality is difficult to define precisely, it almost always includes caring for each other; is always useful, has always involved hard work on someone's part, and when we are involved with it, as either a provider or a receiver, it always feels good. Because it feels so good, I believe all of us carry in our heads a clear idea of what quality is for ourselves.*
> (Glasser, 1992).

In this post-Columbine, post-9/11 era we live in, schooling has taken a more serious tone. Teachers are burdened with roles that go beyond the educators they were trained to become. Strained budgets, overworked staff, state and federal mandates, pressure to increase test scores, deteriorating infrastructure of school buildings, safety protocols, the lessening of parent involvement, and the short-lived career of beginning teachers all add up to serious business. Add to that increased drug, gang, and crime activities and you have the makings for a rerun of the James Cagney film *Opening Day at Alcatraz* rather than the first day of school!

School is a place of learning. Learning should be fun. The perspective of a WOW experience can alter even the direst situations. And all we really have to change is perspective. Changing the first day, the first lesson, the faculty meeting, the parent-teacher conference, the written materials, or the appearance of a school building from dull and serious to something of quality creates a sense of well-being, hope, and motivation. It signals the beginning of something good, even something great. It empowers.

All Abooaarrrddd . . . !

Let's look at how a WOW faculty meeting can meet Dr. Glasser's components of quality. Kevin Kendrick was assistant principal in Meadow Elementary School near Orlando, FL. A new school year was beginning, but on a sour note. The previous year the school struggled to avoid a bad "grade" and did not succeed. They got an "F."

Undeterred in the school's ability to perform, yet conscious the teachers felt challenged and suffered low morale, Kendrick created a WOW he called "Get Aboard the Palmetto Train" which engaged the staff for the year. It began simply enough with a two-week prep time afforded them by the state. They created a train theme for the school year, dragging out old train sets, developing railroad-crossing signs. As they discussed literacy, reading, writing, and math during those two weeks, they blew the train whistle whenever someone said anything good or came up with a "get aboard" idea.

In the beginning of the second week, Kendrick told the teachers they had to be onsite at a certain time, they would be off-campus all day, and they would not be back before 5 p.m. He commandeered two school buses and bussed the teachers to downtown Orlando. They were curious, suspicious, excited, wondering what was going on. Finally they arrived at a train station and up rumbled a 19th-century historic train complete with conductor leaning out the window calling "All abooaarrrddd. . . !" The amazed teachers were grouped on the loading platform, their collective mouths open. They boarded the train and, at 10 miles per hour, chugged for two hours to Mt. Dora, a town replete with antique shops and tearooms.

During the train ride, there was a nearly audible sigh of relief as they relaxed and let the stress of the past week go. They spent the travel time moving from car to car, each with its own focus. One car was a "Getting to Know You Car" where tenured teachers met beginning teachers. Another was a "Goals Car" where a teacher's goals for the year were shared. If they didn't have a goal, they couldn't go to that car.

They arrived at Mt. Dora just in time for lunch and, in keeping with the "Get Aboard the Palmet to Train," teachers broke out of their usual cliques to interact with new faces over lunch. Kendrick, meanwhile, walked around town wearing a tea hat. Teachers were free to browse in shops, relaxing together in a place away from home or school, getting to know one another, and getting aboard the idea that this was a new year at school — one where they would experience quality and would succeed.

In the days following the train ride leading up to the beginning of school, the teaching staff, having now been sufficiently WOWed, spent the remaining prep days discussing how they could WOW their students. The faculty's "Get On Board the Palmetto Train" theme was *their* team's theme. Now it was time for each to create a theme or WOW for their individual classrooms.

Meadow Elementary went from an "F" school to a "C" school that year, and students who couldn't speak English at the beginning of the year were passing the state exams by the end of the year.

Clearly Kevin Kendrick and the school *cared for* the teachers. The event was *useful* in having teachers develop the mindset of getting aboard the new year as well as giving them a chance to communicate and interact in a "third place," away from school or home.

Caring showed as it was involved in *hard work* on the part of the assistant principal in preparing the theme, arranging for the train ride, choosing the destination, setting up events on the various train cars, making sure everyone was included, getting the funding to accomplish the trip. By all accounts, Kendrick was pleased with the event and the teachers *felt good* as a result of this acknowledgment and the surprise of the event.

This event exemplifies the WOW concept. WOW = surprise + quality + purpose. The students walking along a yellow brick road applauded by their teachers and parents surprised them, showed quality in the caring and preparation (hard work). The purpose was to show how welcome they were — a boost in self-esteem for a small child. The WOW was meant to engage them, make them feel wanted, create a positive perspective to learning, and to move them on down the road in their education.

Kemp Elementary School surprised the children and their parents with the flowerpot costumes. A lot of thought and planning went into the first-day WOW, and the school itself had as its theme that year, "Cultivating Success Every Day," so the purpose of the event was to introduce the year's focus.

WOW experiences — quality experiences — need not be limited to students nor the first day of school. Certainly a first-day WOW goes a long way toward generating the motivation to jump into learning in a positive and exciting way. Likewise the first class session, the first staff meeting, the first parent-teacher conference, or parent night sets the stage for a quality experience.

Offering a little extra surprise, something of quality thought out with care, and giving it a purpose creates a WOW experience wherever it falls. What a WOW experience is *not*, however, is entertainment. This is not about teachers entertaining students or principals giving a show for teachers. Certainly an entertaining aspect belongs to WOW events, yet each must be tied to learning or work that follows. Or it can be a culminating experience to anchor learning or tie together a situation once it has occurred, such as a WOW event at the end of a staff meeting.

Flowerpot Quality

In the case of the use of flowerpot hats at Kemp Elementary, for example, the school is the only one in the state certified as a Junior Master Gardener, which makes gardening a part of its quality core curriculum. Teachers knew they were going to teach life science that year. As they planned the opening WOW event for the third grade, they decided to move a culminating unit on plants scheduled for the fall to the beginning of the year to develop a WOW concept from the get-go and achieve buy in and excitement from students year round.

Not only did teachers sport hats decorated as flowerpots, but students were also given unmarked packages of seeds. There were different seeds for different students, and the children were not sure what was in the packages. They shook them, smelled them, and tried to figure out what they had. They were hooked.

Children left for the day with their own flowerpot and seeds and worked with their parents to learn inductively how to plant the seeds. That was their "task" (Note: it was not called homework.) No other directions were given. The growing of these plants, measuring them, doing math associated with their layout, studying their growth, the impact of insects and diseases — all became part of the year's curriculum, all stemming (excuse the pun!) from the initial flowerpot hats and packages of seeds — the opening day WOW.

Beyond creating a learning environment, WOWs resulted in a renewed energy among the teachers and staff, according to Peggy Hollis, principal at Kemp. "We quickly hooked all teachers by asking them to create ways to hook students on the first day with a WOW they could share with their parents," she said. "Teachers gravitated to one another and collaborated to create the first-day WOW. There was a feeling of camaraderie and tremendous motivation. It was contagious." Hollis plans to continue the first-day WOWs and encouraged every teacher to create a first-day-type WOW for every unit. "We will absolutely bring in WOWs for other things throughout the year," concluded Principal Hollis.

Zoom, Zoom, Zoom: A Cautionary Tale

As I work with schools on this concept of WOW, I find I have to caution creative principals and teachers not to get too elaborate with the WOW events. For example, one principal had several friends who raced cars. He scheduled a meeting the day before school opened at the local racetrack. He commandeered a picnic table or two and provided a picnic lunch.

As the teachers ate lunch, the assistant principal gave a little talk about accelerating learning this year. Speeches like this had been given before on the day before school started. But this principal decided he would give the teachers an *experience* of accelerated learning. He and his racecar friends then invited each teacher to get into a racing car where they were then spun around the track in accelerated fashion. Yikes!

As they left the racetrack, one teacher quipped, "Wow. That was great! I can't wait to see what he's going to do *next* year!"

When creating a WOW experience, lesson plan, meeting, conference, or other event, remember to start as you plan to continue — whatever you do the first time will not only be expected, it will be expected to be exceeded. WOW does not have to be huge; WOW can be a simple display of quality, an element of surprise, and an overall purpose for doing it in the first place.

Most importantly, WOW should be fun for the wower and the wowed. Next, we will discover how and *why* to wow.

When Is a WOW a WOW and How Is a WOW Worthwhile?

If WOWs are not meant to be pure entertainment, and they should not be complex and elaborate events destined to take up valuable resources and compete with their own past successes, what functions do they accomplish? What roles do they play in learning and schools?

WOWs serve as precursors to learning. They are the anticipatory set, if you will — the preparation, the inspiration — for a learning experience. They also serve as a mid-course correction when a unit of study gets bogged down or when new knowledge needs to be inserted. WOWs used for debriefing prior learning "sink in" knowledge.

A WOW stimulates learning. It provides novelty. It creates positive emotions. WOWs create an environment for learning. They restore a sense of joy to learning. They are, in short, brain-based. Designed to be multisensory, to stimulate emotions, to be positive, to involve, and to intrigue, WOW experiences signal the brain that something new and exciting is happening. They prime the pump for learning.

What Brain Experts Say

In the foreword to Leslie Hart's updated seminal work *Human Brain & Human Learning,* Dr. M. Donald Thomas, Superintendent of Schools in Salt Lake City says, "The future of teaching and learning lies in the study of the brain. Only in this strange world of nerve cell and synapse will we someday untangle the mysteries of how people learn" (Hart, 1998). Much has been researched, studied, and written about the brain and learning — more in the past 30 years than in all of human history. It's actually caused a learning revolution as brain research sheds light on the need to capture both the intellectual and emotional aspects of the mind. The old Newtonian theory that Nature replicates machines has been replaced by the notion that beyond cognitive learning, the best learning involves the emotions, the body, the senses, learning styles, and creativity.

The school of Accelerated Learning, stemming from work introduced by Bulgarian psychiatrist Georgi Lozanov in the 1970s, led to a movement that embraces brain-based learning and teaching. Resources such as Dave Meier's *The Accelerated Learning Handbook, Accelerated Learning for the 21st Century* by Colin Rose and Malcolm I. Nichol, and *Fire-Up Your Learning* by Thomas L. Madden, M.A., all embrace the concept of capitalizing on how we know the brain works when we learn.

Other advocates of brain-compatible teaching and learning include Leslie Hart as one of its pioneers, Susan Kovalik with her Integrated Thematic Instruction *(ITI: The Model)*, Eric Jensen and his multiple books on the brain and learning, including *Teaching with the Brain in Mind, Brain-Based Learning and Teaching*, and *The Learning Brain*, and Robert Sylwester and his *Celebration of Neurons.* All speak to the value of including stimulating and motivating techniques in teaching.

Mind-Body Events
Naturally WOW Us

WOWs fall right into the category of stimulating learning. According to Arnold Scheibel, Ph.D., director of brain research, the University of California Los Angeles, "unfamiliar activities are the brain's best friend" (Scheibel, 1994). The brain is stimulated by novelty, and Scheibel theorizes it might be a survival response. Without it, we may never have left the cave. Something new stimulates the brain to move out of its routine thinking; new dendrites are created, branching out. Synapses are formed, and the brain grows. Growing is what the brain does for survival. Lack of stimulation atrophies the brain. "The brain grows with use and withers with disuse" (Scheibel, 1999).

The theories of Accelerated Learning and Neuro-Linguistic Programming (NLP) focus on elements that alert the brain to perk up; they tell it something is happening. Time to learn. NLP ties movement and emotions to action, decisions, and learning. It anchors learning through experiential body and mind focus points.

Accelerated Learning proves learning is a whole-mind-body event. The event is creative. As the brain creates new meanings, it makes sense of whatever new has occurred — in the case of WOWs, the surprise factor. WOWs are often multisensory and involve all learning styles.

WOWed on the Spot

WOWs work when people get involved in the WOW activity itself. People learn in the context of what they are doing. How often have you left a room to get a book or other item, forgotten what you were after when you left, and then as you returned to the spot where you had the thought, you remembered it? That is because the brain always knows where it was when learning occurred. The thought was in the context of that room. Likewise, if a student is involved in a WOW experience, the memory of what occurred in that experience and where it occurred stays with the student.

Because they represent quality, WOWs embrace positive emotions. According to Dave Meier (2000), "Learning that is stressful, painful, and dreary can't hold a candle to learning that is joyful, relaxed, and engaging." WOW introduces a feeling of joy, and joy serves as a magic platform for learning.

Anatomy of a Brain-Based WOW and the Veiled Chameleon

Yet WOWs in and of themselves are not necessarily learning experiences. They shore up learning, whether before, during, or after the lesson learned. Let's look first at how WOWs serve as preparation for learning. The first step is to arouse interest. WOWs arouse curiosity. They evoke a natural childlike state of openness, freedom, anticipation, intrigue, and suspense.

Science Resource teacher Richard Ellenburg sees all 1,400 K-5 students over a course of two weeks at Camelot Elementary School in Orlando, FL. Always seeking to arouse interest in his Science Resource class, Ellenburg inaugurates each class with a WOW on the first day.

For starters, Ellenburg's classroom sports several aquariums, an earthworm farm, and box turtles walk around the classroom. Both a Ball Python and a Red Rat Snake call his classroom home, and he is currently raising Leopard Geckos. A pair of canaries sing and a tall aviary houses four families of finches. Two rabbits inhabit the garden outside the classroom. He and his students watch caterpillars form chrysalises and then morph into butterflies. The butterflies are released on a regular basis. A mini-museum of clear plastic boxes containing snakeskin, fossils, rocks, and other detritus of nature lines a shelf that encompasses the room.

As if that's not enough to intrigue kids from kindergarten to fifth grade, Ellenburg starts the first day of class by letting his Veiled Chameleon catch live crickets. A Veiled Chameleon has a tongue that shoots out 6 to 8 inches as it snaps up its prey. (If your mind is going to Budweiser® commercials, you get the picture.)

The teacher sits on a chair, strumming his guitar quietly to set the tone. Students are gathered there, but their heads are twisting around taking in the zoo-like atmosphere. There is tremendous excitement and anticipation. Then Ellenburg brings out the Veiled Chameleon and asks if anyone wants to feed it. The selected child holds a cricket, and the chameleon flicks it out of his hand. Squeals of laughter and awe erupt. "Do it again!" So he does.

Ellenburg then puts the chameleon on his head and talks about where the chameleon originated in Madagascar and how fragile he is. Then he puts the chameleon back into the aquarium and washes his hands with antibacterial soap. He cautions any student who handled the crickets to wash his or her hands with the antibacterial soap as well.

The lesson about hygiene and hand washing segues into a discussion about the rules of the room — how they are guests of the animals in the room. How they do not disturb the animals, they don't lean on aquariums, or feed the animals. How to be courteous and respectful to the animals while keeping safe. Then he lets them wander and peek and meld into this classroom of wonders to be unearthed.

Reptiles eating crickets in and of itself may not be learning, except in a perceptual way. Using that to trigger interest, to arouse the student's brain into wanting to know more — oh-so-much more — is both brain-based and WOW-based learning. As much fun as that classroom allows, it uses all the fun stuff to shore up the learning. This is a live science lab, a garden classroom, and a place where the interest to be scientists is created.

WOWs Segue to Brain-Based Learning

Step one then is to arouse curiosity with a WOW experience. That WOW event leads to new information, knowledge, or skill. Once learned, there must be practice or integration of the knowledge, and that leads to performance or application of the knowledge. All four of these components of brain-based learning need to occur for learning to occur.

The WOW is the preparation to get learners into an active state, out of resistance or passivity. It is a kick-start to learning. The WOW softens the obstacles to learning that students often bear — indifference, feeling of boredom as well as fear of failure, change, or ridicule. Everyone's in the WOW together. Everyone experiences the surprise, the quality, and the purpose, so the threat of learning is dissolved.

This then creates a positive forward-moving step toward learning. The WOW inspires it. It brings people out of their resistances, passivity, hostility, or isolation and into the moment. A WOW also focuses on the positive of learning — how good the learning will be. This is going to be fun, interesting. You're in for a treat. You will learn quickly, and you'll be amazed what you'll be able to do. You will receive incredible value. You're in the arms of quality, and you are the beneficiary. (How different from "we have a lot of material to cover this year and not very much time" or "you may not understand all of this, but at least try.")

Of course WOWs do not guarantee learning. They are, however, solidly based in research showing that the brain will be activated to learn. Similar to using starting activities in cooperative learning, developing live-event learning activities, going on field trips, applying integrated thematic instruction, or creating brain-compatible classrooms, WOWs provide a safe space for the brain to entertain a sense of body-mind connectedness, involvement with others, enjoyment, a relaxed sense of peace and, yes, joy.

Later we'll look at how WOWs can be used not only to arouse curiosity at the beginning of learning, but also to create "state changes" — another brain-based element — and celebrations of learning.

First, Do a WOW

Children have long understood the value of a WOW experience. One could say young children live in the WOW. In the early days of "show and tell," WOW experiences were had daily. Creating WOWs purposefully allows teachers and students alike to don a childlike state of wonder and excitement. WOWs are important to arouse curiosity and motivate learning, and they can be used intermittently throughout the year in a variety of ways.

Beginning a new year, a new unit of study, a new subject, or a new procedure with a WOW creates the strongest of impressions. There is an old adage: "You don't get a second chance to make a first impression." Creating a WOW at the beginning of school sets the stage for the entire year. It intrigues and motivates, and it also sets a standard.

Start with quality, and you have automatically developed a benchmark from which you can operate. You can outdo yourself; students can chip in to help make learning a WOW experience. It's like a game where everyone wins.

Here are some examples of first-day WOWs.

First-Day WOWs

A Briefcase Full of Money

A vocational education teacher enters the room on the first day of class carrying an official looking leather briefcase complete with handle and locking hasps. He sets the briefcase flat on the desk and begins talking to the students. In a droning monotone, the teacher points out that this voc-ed program is very beneficial, but at times it may be boring. There will be lots of work to do, and it's going to be hard, awfully hard.

As the students' eyes begin to glaze over, their bodies' shift, and their feet shuffle uncomfortably. The teacher abruptly stops and asks in a loud voice, "Why are you here?!" Students look to one another surprised and a little shocked at his shift in tone, some perhaps wondering why, indeed, they *are* there.

Then the teacher snaps open the briefcase loudly. He tips it so students can see that it is full to the brim with neat stacks of money — $20 bills in many bundles, two layers deep.[1] Each bundle is secured by a rubber band. The students gasp.

"Well," continues the teacher, now smiling, "You're here because this is the kind of money you can earn if you are qualified in this program," and he slowly thumbs through a bundle grinning at the students who are now completely engaged and awestruck.

Welcome to Summer School!

Summer session in a middle school in inner-city Philadelphia began with children arriving on foot, by public transportation, or dropped off by their parents. They started up a large staircase toward the library. Lining the steps were teachers greeting them as they choose among high fives, smiles, shaking hands, applause.

---

[1] Before you go out to rob a bank, note that this teacher used one of the oldest gangster tricks in the world. He placed a $20 bill on the top and on the bottom of each bundle were cut up newspapers that served as unseen fillers.

Once in the library, teachers positioned themselves in chorus-line fashion as students were seated. They began singing the Temptations' "The Way You Do the Things You Do," acting out the various parts of the song. Students felt welcome; teachers bonded as a team.

Trailer Trash: A Cinderella Story

Overflowing schools often rent or purchase portable classrooms called "modules" that are parked on the school campus, usually on or near a parking lot away from the main building. Despite what they call them, these vehicles look and act like trailers. In one elementary school in the Midwest — and probably in others nationwide — students whose teachers are assigned to teach in the portable modules are cruelly called "trailer trash" and are teased by others who attend classes in the main building.

On the first day of school, those students assigned to attend class in one of these trailers climbed inside to discover a woman standing there in a dirty housecoat and slippers. There were curlers in her messy hair, and she had several teeth missing as evidenced by the black spaces between them.

She welcomed the students into the module, "Come on in and set right down!" she said, plopping herself down on a chair, swinging her slipper-clad foot up and down, as she gently picked at her teeth with a toothpick. The young children did as they were told and stared at this odd-looking teacher, wondering what was coming next.

Suddenly the teacher stood up, grinned broadly, and said, "Welcome to our trailer! We are going to have *so much FUN* here this year, you just wait and see!"

She turned her back to the students, repeating how they were going to have a wonderful school year and, as she talked, quickly pulled the black licorice off her teeth, unbuttoned the front of her housecoat, turned around and let it drop to the floor. Underneath, she was wearing a beautiful long, gold-sequined gown. She yanked out the hair curlers and tousled her hair; then she tossed off her slippers and put on matching sequined high heels. The transformation from "Wicked Witch" to "Fairy Godmother" was magical.

"You see?" she said. "You never know what someone or something is until you look *underneath* it. You think this is a trailer, but it's *not*," she lowered her voice, looking furtively out the window of the trailer in case someone outside was listening. "This is a Magic Pumpkin," she said loudly, smiling. "This is *not* a trailer! And we are going to learn so much and have so much fun all year long in our Magic Pumpkin that all the other kids will be very jealous of us."

Students were smiling and clapping, happily wowed and reassured.

Brass Bands and Zany Welcome Packets

Another school asked the high school brass band to play as students entered the auditorium on the first day, a hired clown greeting them at the door.

A WOW that gains momentum occurs by sending a packet to students prior to the first day. The packet would be colorful, zany, upbeat, and informative. In it, the student could be assigned a nickname or a name in a category, such as a car brand or flower or baseball team. On arrival, they enter into a collaborative learning environment as they seek to find other cars or flowers or baseball teams of the same name.

WOWs from A to Z

First-day WOWs run the gamut from A to Z. They can be simple or elaborate. They focus on the idea that this is going to be an experience that may surprise you, please you (quality), and that has as its purpose:

a) to welcome you.

b) to indicate the theme of the year.

c) to entice you to want to know more.

d) to segue to learning.

e) to make you laugh.

f) to ease your stress.

g) to indicate school is a friendly place.

h) to create suspense.

i) to eliminate doubts or fears.

j) to acknowledge you.

k) to boost your self-esteem.

l) to temporarily confuse you.

m) to accept you.

n) to give you a sense of security.

o) to intrigue you.

p) to activate your brain.

q) to let you anticipate.

r) to involve your whole mind and body.

s) to start on a positive note.

t) to "upshift" you into a learning space.

u) to prepare you for a quality year.

v) to get you out of isolation.

w) to give you the big picture.

x) to make you proud of your school.

y) to make you proud of yourself.

z) to WOW you!!

Emotional Brain, Intellectual Brain

All of these purposes and the context of WOW can be experienced in a whole-school mode or in the individual classrooms. Dr. Brenda Stallion taught undergraduates aspiring to be high school teachers at Western Kentucky University in Bowling Green, KY. Every year she divided students into "departments" that correlated with most high school subjects: social studies, English, math, science, American literature, Spanish, or other foreign language.

Part and parcel of every class included the need to develop "a first-day *content-driven* motivational WOW" that would tie into their academic topics. In asking them to develop these activities, Dr. Stallion taught the difference between the affective and effective management techniques of teaching — engagement and management.

Here to the rescue once again comes the brain. Using a business-based book *You Have to Be Believed to Be Heard* by Bert Decker, Stallion's class learned about the emotional brain and the intellectual brain. While it is doubtful our marvelous brains are simply divided into "right" and "left" as once thought — but rather work as a whole complex organism — Decker points to research that shows the older part of the brain (in terms of historical development) contains the seat of emotions.

This part of the brain developed for survival, instinctual responses, and houses the emotional center — where we might find our "emotional intelligence."

Decker defines the more intellectual part of the brain as the cerebral cortex governing conscious thought, memory, language, decision-making, and creativity. This brain surrounds and protects the older region that generates emotions, feelings, subconscious thoughts, hunger, thirst, sexuality, and parental care. His point is we all possess the ability to respond to new information or learning both emotionally, usually first, and then logically or intellectually.

So where does the WOW fit in? The WOW moves first to attract and communicate with the more emotional part of our brain. That is the affective aspect, and WOWs motivate that emotional portion of the brain in order to get to the more intellectual part. While we can address the intellectual brain and impart cognitive knowledge, we may not really communicate without first engaging the emotions. And a WOW does that.

Heeeeerrreeeezz Elvis!

Dr. Stallion's class created first-day WOWs that some videotaped and all wrote up in a narrative. In American Literature, students dressed in costumes representing various characters their students would be learning about during the year. The Social Studies "department" invoked not only figures from the past such as Abraham Lincoln, a cowboy, Native American, Marilyn Monroe, Richard Nixon, and others, but also created a live Elvis Presley to interview them!

No matter the WOW, the bridge to what that year's learning was going to focus on dominated — the bridge from the emotional brain enjoying the WOW to the intellectual brain learning who and what and why and how.

WOWS That Keep On WOWing

Some first-day WOWs both engage students and can be referred to periodically throughout the school year to refocus and remind students about their purpose. Since WOWs on the first day of school or at a first class session are memorable, some can be stretched as a theme or reminder of that first day to serve as a sort of "re-wowal." You don't want to belabor a really good opening WOW that has already served its purpose, yet some lend themselves to a certain amount of repetition, like the chorus of a good ballad. Here are some examples.

The Snapping Dollar Bill

As high school math students enter the classroom, their teacher hands each of them a dollar bill. That's a WOW right there.

They take their seats, and the teacher takes another dollar bill and jerks it tightly by pulling on either end, creating a loud snapping sound. He does this a few times as students watch and listen.

"You all received a dollar bill," he points out sternly. "If you pass this class, you get to keep it. If you do *not* pass this class, you have to pay me interest on the dollar bill." Students are a little taken aback, curious, intrigued.

"You have to pay back the dollar bill," he repeats, "with interest compounded *daily*." Now students look to one another to see if anyone comprehends this.

"Uh," says one student, "like, how much would that be?"

"Ah," says the teacher, smiling. "So glad you asked!" And so begins the first math lesson.

Throughout the school year, if students working in groups are struggling over a problem for which no one seems to have an answer, the teacher walks among them, snapping the dollar bill as a reminder to keep working, figure it out. When a student forgets his or her homework, he snaps the dollar again, saying, "Pay attention! This could get expensive!"

The Gift Box

Another math WOW occurred in an elementary school. On the first day, the teacher has someone deliver a large box. It's gift-wrapped with a huge bow. It looks like a really nice gift — big, square, pretty.

"Wow," the students exclaim. "Is that for us? What is it? Can we open it?" They're all talking at once.

The teacher says it certainly is for them and they can open it but first they need to find out its *volume*.

"How do we know what that is?" says one anxious child.

"Well, we need to look it up in the math book," suggests the teacher. "Let's turn to page 8."

The opening WOW immediately segues into a math lesson as students learn about volume. They measure the length and width of the box and learn about measurement. Then fractions.

In a couple weeks, the students learn the entire math necessary to determine the volume of the box.

They have covered all the elements and the box remains nicely wrapped on a table in the room.

When they finally have the volume, the teacher creates an important ceremony around opening the box. Inside, there is a long string of candy rolled round and round in a plastic bag. The students clap their hands gleefully. But wait! On top of the string of candy is a note. It says, "You can eat me when you can divide me evenly among yourselves."

Off to the math book again . . . .

Survival Kit

A sixth-grade English class begins with a teacher dressed in camouflage gear.

"Okay," students wonder, "what are we in for *now*?"

On each student's desk rests a small nylon bag with a zipper and a handle. Adhered to the top of each bag is a wide white tape with words in block letters "SIXTH GRADE SURVIVAL KIT."

The teacher stands straight and stiff before the class, hands on hips military style, and directs the students to become acquainted with their Survival Kits — to unzip them and check the contents carefully.

They do so and find a compass, a small flashlight, a Band-Aid®, and a pack of Lifesaver® candies. "Huh?" the students wonder, intrigued.

"Welcome to 'Surviving Sixth Grade'!" says the teacher, hands still on hips but smiling now. "We are going to work on the beautiful skill of creative writing," she smiles. "That is sometimes nerve-wracking for some, and yet I want you to survive and succeed in this class, so you can use this Survival Kit throughout the year to ensure you complete the mission of learning how to write well," she adds.

"What are these things for?" the students ask.

"The compass is to help you find the direction you want to take with your writing," says the teacher. "Each piece you write will have its own direction, its own plot and theme.

"The Lifesavers are there when you need help. I will always be available to you to help and guide you through the writing process."

"What about the Band-Aid?" asks one student.

"Ah. These are very handy," the teacher responds. "You see, when correcting your writing, I use a red pen. Some think the papers I return look downright bloody. So the Band-Aid can be used as your safety valve. You can place the Band-Aid right over a grade that really disturbs you — the grade that may accompany a red-splotchy paper."

"Cool," says another student. "How often can we do that?"

"Just once," says the teacher, smiling. "We all have some writing we're not truly proud of. The 'muse' just didn't happen or we got tangled up in the story. That's not the end of the world and I want you to have another chance, so if you put a Band-Aid on a paper you're not crazy about, I'll eliminate the grade."

"Wow," whisper the students. "That's awesome."

In the back of the classroom, there are logs stacked up with a glow from a light underneath them. Cushions and low-backed chairs are all around the logs. The whole scene resembles a cozy campfire. The teacher asks them to take their flashlights and go arrange themselves around the campfire. She dims the lights in the classroom, picks up a book, and proceeds to settle down with them to begin reading from the first creative writing book.

Throughout the year, the students use their Survival Kit to ask for direction, help, assistance, and to camouflage the grade on that really *bad* story they wrote. Whenever a new book or topic is introduced, the teacher asks them to grab their flashlights and join her at the campfire glowing (from a hidden flashlight) at the back of the room.

A gift — a WOW — that keeps on giving.

We Didn't Start the Fire

Ruth Angert has taught for 28 years, most recently at Gaither High School in Tampa, FL. Like many teachers, she began her first day of school going over the rules for the year. After attending a session where I lamented about the lack of WOWs for students on the first day, a light bulb went on in Ruth's head.

A teacher of social studies and American history — advanced placement, honors, and regular classes —Ruth typically developed rich, multi-sensory lessons throughout the year. She included musicals, "history alive" lessons, and other engaging activities — but never on the first day of school.

She racked her brain to see what she could do to give students a first-day WOW. She recalled a song by Billy Joel, "We Didn't Start the Fire," recounting historical events and characters from 1949 to 1989 — people and places and events such as North and South Korea, Walter Winchell, Eisenhower, vaccine, Davy Crockett, hula hoops,

Hemingway, Malcolm X, Bay of Pigs, birth control, Woodstock, Watergate, and so forth. The chorus proclaims:

We didn't start the fire.

It was always burning

Since the world's been turning

We didn't start the fire.

No, we didn't light it

But we tried to fight it.

We didn't start the fire

But when we are gone,

Will it still burn on, and on, and on, and on . . . ?

Ruth used the song on the first day of all her social studies and American history classes. She found an old audiocassette of the song and a large boombox. She wrote the words to the entire song on her whiteboard and played the music loudly as students marched in, curious and excited. She used the song to point out that students were going to study these people and events throughout the school year. They were engaged. She got a WOW.

But Ruth wasn't satisfied with just one WOW, so she pulled out a dollar bill and asked students to do the same. Those who didn't have one were provided one (wow!). She showed them the parts of the dollar, its material, symbols, plus the Latin and English wording. Then she asked them to turn it over and look at the pyramid on the back. She asked them to notice that the pyramid was unfinished, and they all discussed why. As she covered the elements of the dollar bill, she referenced it back to the song and then segued into a history or social studies lesson.

So, a double WOWee for Ruth.

And it didn't end there. Students learned the words to Billy Joel's song and sang it back and forth to each other all year. The honors class did research and wrote the next stanza of the song to bring it from 1990 to the present. They made posters of their stanza to exhibit what it meant. They illustrated it. They presented it to others. Parents came to the open house and asked to hear the song. Ruth played it for them. Students went online and searched for "We Didn't Start the Fire" and learned about a kid who took the song and made pictures to match every word.

"I will *never* cover rules the first day of school again!" Ruth proclaimed. "Starting with the song was so exciting for me and for the students. I've been teaching a long time, and it made me realize that something simple like that, catching them with a WOW the first day, was amazing and powerful."

In these WOW stories and many others occurring across the country, it is vital to remember that the WOW empowers students to choose to learn. WOWs are not about "we have them do this," or "we make them do that." WOWs arouse; they don't manipulate. The WOW is a tease, an invitation, or a kick-start that students can use to move them into the realm of learning something new.

And what about teachers? As Kevin Kendrick showed us in his "Get Aboard the Palmetto Train" WOW, and the principal proved in scooting his teachers around a racetrack, teachers need emWOWerment, too! Beth Provancha, a principal at both Conway and Corner Lakes Middle Schools in Orange County, FL, understood fully the value of WOWing teachers. At both middle schools, Pavancha created a WOW event teachers recall to this day.

WOWs and Teachers: The Autograph WOW

The faculty was to meet at the media center for the first day of pre-planning. As they approached the entrance of the building, they were amazed to see a long red carpet on the walkway from parking lot to school entrance. Braided velvet barriers held up by brass poles paraded on either side of the bright red carpet reminiscent of those used at the Academy Awards to guide movie stars into the glittering hall.

Behind the braided velvet barrier were parents and students dressed gaudily as tourists. As the teachers approached, parents and students treated them as celebrities, clicking their cameras like paparazzi and holding out books, asking teachers for their autographs. "Oh, you're a teacher! How wonderful! May I have your autograph?" Some screamed and feigned swooning.

Inside, Provancha debriefed the WOW experience with the teachers once their blood pressure had returned to normal. Each then created a WOW they shared with students on the first day of class. One started his social studies class dressed as a knight in King Arthur's Court. Another donned Colonial garb and insisted everyone in her gifted social studies class call her "Mistress Nix."

Cheryl Wood, Senior Administrator of Instruction at the Professional Development Services in Orange County Public Schools, was a teacher at the time with Provancha. She said, "It was a morale booster for the entire staff. We began validating each other's attempt to do something in the classroom that was different. It was fun. We kept saying 'WOW!' to one another." Cheryl herself brought in a rope of lights, formed it into the word WOW, and put it on the wall in her office. She left it up and turned on all year long.

Wow!

WOWing Up Learning

Funeral for I Can'ts

WOWS aren't just for first days. They can be for any new beginning. Jacquelyn Sweetner Caffey is a remedial reading teacher at Davison Elementary School in Detroit, MI. Caffey focuses her lessons first on her children's self-esteem, knowing it paves the way for learning how to read.

On the videotape *The Truth About Teachers*[1], one finds Caffey teaching a class while wearing a black dress and a felt hat with a black veil. At the front of

[1] VHS videotape about real K-12 teachers hosted by Whoopi Goldberg (1989).

the room lies a large bucket, also black. Behind her a sign reads, "Last rites for the Late Mr. I Can't."

Caffey has created a funeral setting where she intends to bury any "I can'ts" her students have about reading. Each student completes a form that states, "I can't _____ as well as some of my classmates." Each student fills in the blank. Most put "read." They repeat the process with another form and another "I can't."

Then Ms. Caffey asks them to fold the "I can'ts" in half and then in half again. The students take their folded sheets and march to the front of the class and drop their "I can'ts" into the bucket as Caffey sings and claps a funeral dirge.

"Now," she says, "those 'I Can'ts' are gone and we aren't *ever* going to hear them anymore in this classroom or anywhere else either!" Then she commences to teach them how to read.

The Mad Scientist

Richard Ellenburg of Camelot Elementary School in Orange County, FL, comes to school in a white lab coat down to his ankles, a hard hat, huge gloves reaching to his elbows, a pair of goggles, and a pocket protector. He asks his students, "Who am I?" They respond, "A scientist!"

He places a tub of found materials on tables in the classroom. There are parts from discarded VCRs and computers and simple machines with pulleys. The children explore the tubs and ask questions. Ellenburg points out that what they are doing — exploring — is just what a scientist does!

He gives them rulers to measure the piles, to learn how big or wide or tall some items are. Then he says, "Well, I'll be! That's exactly what *scientists* do: investigate!"

Next, he brings them books to look through. Why? Well scientists do research, he points out, and we will do research. "Say," he smiles, "I'll be! We're ALL scientists!"

He claims that by the end of the session, every student wants to be a scientist when he or she grows up.

Writing on the Wall

Andrea Schmidt, AP and honors chemistry teacher at Clearview Regional High School in New Jersey, intrigues her sometimes-intimidated chemistry students by writing on the wall — with invisible ink! She creates a chemical solution and paints words and phrases on a poster board. But you can only read them when the board is wet. Once dry, the posters are posted on the wall and look completely blank.

After students arrive and class is underway, she takes another chemical and sprays it onto the poster board, and what she has written becomes visible as if by magic. Some of her phrases include: "Chem-Is Try," and "Schmidt is the best!" and "You're going to have fun with chemistry." Of course, they all want to know how it's done[1] and she lets them try it for themselves.

The Sounds of Silence

Lest you think all WOWs have to be funny, let's peek into an eighth-grade English classroom in Mullica Hill, NJ. Here teacher Barbie Pagano asks her class what they like to do when they're stuck at home on a rainy day with their brothers or sisters. Students share some of their activities. Ms. Pagano reveals that she and her brother played "Hungry, Hungry Hippos" and asks if they would like to play. They do.

She brings out a four-person board game. It includes four hippo heads with large mouths, a handle on each of the four sides of the game board

[1] To prepare the two different solutions, dissolve 1 g NH_4 SCN in 100 ml H_2O, and 4.0 g $K_4Fe(CN)_6$ €$3H_2O$ in 100 ml H_2O. The spray that will make them visible is prepared by dissolving 6.75 g $FeCl_3$ €$6H_2O$ in 250 ml water.

that directs each hippo head, and a whole slew of marbles placed in the center of the board. The object is to have each person's hippo "eat" as many marbles as possible — all at once, fast — ready, set go! It's exciting, it's fun, and everyone wants to play.

Then Ms. Pagano asks them to play the game without making any noise. If anyone makes noise, those watching bust them. They soon learn it's impossible to play the game without any noise.

Pagano then opens a can of soda and a bag of chips. She hands another can and bag to a student and asks him to open it silently. It can't be done. She walks on a sample of hardwood flooring she brought in and asks them to do the same. She admonishes them to walk without any noise at all, silently. By now the students are curious, a little frustrated, confused.

At that point, Barbie Pagano segues into the story of Anne Frank, who needed to remain quiet, interacting with siblings and relatives for long, boring stretches at a time, completely silent. From the students' experience of what it must have been like to operate in silence, they are eager, ready, empathetic, intrigued, and excited to begin reading *The Diary of Anne Frank*.

WOWs Versus Good Lessons

Are those WOWs or just good units of study, clever lessons? Well, the designation of what is a WOW gets a bit wobbly when it comes to lessons. Teachers across the country constantly develop creative lesson plans designed to get sustained attention from students. So isn't a good lesson a WOW?

Not exactly. WOWs do share with lessons the purpose of learning, but they also exemplify quality. We learned from Dr. William Glasser in Chapter One, quality "almost always includes caring for each other; is always useful, has always involved hard work on someone's part, and when we are involved with it, as either a provider or a receiver, it always feels good" (Glasser, 1992), and although some lesson plans work well and are used over and over again, in my experience, they do not necessarily contain all the elements of quality.

Moreover, WOWs have an element of surprise, novelty. They're out of context. They're fun, new, light, and bring a sense of wonder. WOWs might also create anticipation, suspense, and curiosity — even confusion over what's going on, the unknown.

This element of being out of context, adding surprise and wonder and emotion tends to set WOWs apart from lesson plans, even dynamic lesson plans. WOW experiences are *short-lived*. It is difficult to be novel or sustain a state of surprise, wonder, or even fun over a long period of time. Once the WOW is over, there is opportunity to move on to a learning experience with quality — a creative lesson plan that develops learning and shows caring, is useful, involves hard work, and feels good.

Brain-Based State Changes

WOWs definitely belong right alongside great lesson plans. WOWs create *state changes*, an important brain-based element that underscores the value of peppering learning with periodic WOWs. A state change consists of a body-mind movement that actually creates a chemical balance in the body (Jensen, 1997). It signals to the brain that a new learning experience is beginning. It shifts the focus from what was happening to what will be.

State changes occur by creating thoughts and suggested mental pictures, by moving the body, breathing, gestures, activities, change in environment. In the film *Dead Poets' Society*, Robin Williams plays John Keating, a professor of poetry in a snooty boys' prep school in New England. To keep the interest of students, Keating creates imaginative and humorous state changes each time a new poem, poet, lesson, or historical period is covered.

His "first day" WOW consists of his wandering through the classroom where the boys are seated neatly in shirts and ties. He whistles as he wanders and beckons them into the hallway without having uttered a word.

They all look curiously at one another as if to say, "*this* is different" and then they grab their books, get up, and follow him out of the room. He asks them to look in the glass case in the hallway showing old photos of students who graduated many years prior and who are now long dead.

The camera moves from a close up of a student in a black-and-white photo to a close up of a student in Keating's class who looks an awful lot like the one in the photo and, by his expression, he knows that too. As the students gaze at the photos of dead students, Keating eerily moves among them as they stand grouped before the glass asking in a deep voice what will *their* lives be like, admonishing them then in a slow, eerie whisper, as if ghosts of the former students, *"Car-pe di-em . . . seizzze the daaaaay."*

Later students are seen marching around a courtyard to understand the tendency to conform. In another scene, they stand up on their desks to gain perspective.

These are examples of state changes. They can be as simple as asking students to get up and move to a different desk or location. They include a change of scenery, the introduction of music, suddenly turning the lights off or on, asking students to stand up and stretch, or requesting they turn around and share with the person behind them what they ate for breakfast.

Just as WOWs are powerful at the beginning of school or the beginning of a class, so too are they powerful as a state change, at the beginning of a new phase or new subject or new facet of learning. In longer units of study, there can be many WOWs signaling the shift to another level of learning.

Priming the Pump

In *Meaningful Activities to Generate Interesting Classrooms*®, a graduate course developed by Performance Learning Systems, Inc., course designer Charles Young calls beginning activities that introduce the day or a new facet of learning "priming the pump." He suggests enticing students to learn by first creating something fun or curious, much as we do with WOWs.

He describes a teacher who hangs various signs on the door of his classroom, such as "Special Event for Today," or "Mr. Wizard Says He Can Prove that One and One *Doesn't* Equal Two!" This intrigues students entering class, makes them curious. Another teacher hangs lesson-related signs around the room, possibly referencing historical events or language arts or science, making students wonder what it's all about.

The Magical Banana

Performing magic tricks highlights the impact of a WOW. Young describes a fifth-grade teacher who uses a banana story to talk about Mayan Indian cultures. First, he paints a verbal picture of the Mayan Indians in Cancun on the Yucatan Peninsula of Mexico. He intrigues his students by describing the scene, people living in houses of bamboo with straw roofs and dirt floors, chickens running in the streets. He points out that long ago the Mayans made great intellectual advances, such as using a precise system of writing and developing an accurate calendar based on a high level of mathematics.

The teacher then shares that the one thing that really fascinated him was when he learned the Mayans had developed a magical banana. This magical banana is already sliced inside its peel! The Mayans developed this magical already-sliced banana so they could put it on their cereal more quickly.

Then the teacher takes a banana, peels it, and they are WOWed by the fact that it is, in fact, already sliced!

The trick is to take a ripe banana, insert a long pin into one of its veins, and slice through the flesh of the banana horizontally, but not through the skin. Do this at half-inch intervals down the length of the banana by inserting the pin numerous times. Of course, the banana "trick" is done ahead of when the class meets, and well worth the WOW, often preceded by "NO WAY!"

Games, mental exercises, or other activities are also a part of a WOW but, once again, to be a WOW activity they need to tie to learning, show quality, and contain an element of surprise, fun, wonder, or novelty. A good WOW can keep students engaged in the classroom all year long. Here's one example.

Global Virtual Tour

On the first day of his social studies class, Clearview Regional High School teacher Joe Sullivan tells his students they will not be remaining in the classroom. As students look confused, he explains all will be going on a Global Virtual Tour all year long.

The teacher puts an empty fishbowl on his desk and announces he will be holding a lottery, only it's not for money. It's for a trip around the world. Students draw lottery tickets for five locations on any of the inhabited continents of the world. They are challenged to create a Global Virtual Tour for the rest of the semester to and from their location.

Teams of three to four students are formed and initially plot a trip from Mullica Hill, NJ, where the school is located, to their five destinations and back again. They trace their route on a hand-drawn world map that shows the distances traveled and the time they will spend flying.

To enrich this Global Virtual Tour, students study each country. They make posters, create climographs showing the average monthly temperature and rainfall. They produce artifacts and interesting ways of demonstrating the country. They create T-shirts, make foods indigenous to the country. Ultimately all the students' work ends in demonstrations and a museum viewed by other students, teachers, and parents at the end of the school year.

"That was the nicest thing I've done in 30 years," says Sullivan. "Every kid was involved — even some of the academically challenged kids. All learning styles were engaged. Everyone did well. I was more pleased with the results of the Global Virtual Tour than almost any other thing I could think of." The excitement of the lottery for a world tour primed the pump.

Here are some examples of other lessons that are enriched by novelty, surprise, fun, or the "warm fuzzies" of a WOW.

Tongue Twisters

Students in a middle school English class are preparing for an oral presentation. They are nervous.

They rehearse with one another but forget whole passages. They become frustrated.

Suddenly their teacher jumps up and goes to the front of the room where she proceeds to loudly recite *Fox in Sox* by Dr. Seuss, a tongue-twisting book by any standard. She speaks in a high-pitched voice. She stumbles over the words, makes silly mistakes, laughs in the middle. That allows the students to laugh, feel all right, and know that making mistakes is part of the process.

Balloon Races

A middle school science teacher starts his class off by blowing up a balloon with cut up straws. He says nothing. As students watch, the teacher blows up one balloon and then another. He ties them off and tosses them into the classroom. Students look to one another as if to say, "What's with this guy?"

The teacher then asks his students to cut some straws and blow up balloons of their own. They do what he says, by now wondering if their teacher is a sandwich short of a picnic.

The teacher laughs and becomes the science teacher they were expecting. He shows them how to string fishing line across the room to which to affix their balloons, and announces they will be having a balloon race, but first they must measure the circumference of the balloons and figure out their velocity. They learn what each of those terms means and how to make calculations. With the teacher's guidance, they graph the circumference versus the velocity and determine the best circumference to get maximum velocity. Maximum velocity, of course, wins balloon races.

Once the lesson is completed, "Ready, Set, GO!" They're free to race their balloons. So they do.

Spanish Fiesta

A WOW activity for a Spanish class was developed by a group of undergraduates. They suggested greeting students at the beginning of a year of Spanish class wearing costumes that depict fashions from a Spanish-speaking culture. They welcome students by speaking to them in Spanish.

The classroom has been decorated to resemble a plaza ready for a fiesta. There are booths with food; someone is playing a guitar. There is a small model of a fountain in the middle to replicate a piazza. The room is rimmed with booths showing geography exhibits, a map showing Spanish-speaking countries, food and culture, music. Someone is performing a Spanish folk dance. All the while, the "teachers" are letting their students know how much fun they will be having in this exciting Spanish class.

Ole!

WOW it Forward

The acid test of any WOW, of course, occurs when the WOWee says so. Young children achieve that sense of wonder and excitement from seemingly simple pleasures — a butterfly lands on them, they discover a "treasure"; a fireplug bursts and sprays water on the sidewalk on a hot day.

Theme park owners have been in the WOW business for a long time, continually looking for bigger and better ways to attract tourists. As we get older, it takes a little more effort to WOW us. Yet I believe there exists that child within us that resonates with quality. When someone takes the time to create a WOW experience — when they show that much caring — it is really the same as giving a gift. "I thought you'd get a kick out of this, so I . . . ." "Come on, let's surprise Sally by . . . ." "I know what let's do! When they come in the door, we'll . . . ."

The brain-based elements of a WOW remain a constant regardless of age or circumstance. As long as we continue to have a brain, it will be stimulated by novelty, relationship, color, music, sensory stimuli, meaning, emotion, and relevancy. And the brain perks up when there are choices, where the environment feels safe. After a WOW occurs, there's time to laugh and debrief what happened — to get the immediate feedback our brains crave and from which they grow.

Side Benefits of WOWs

Keeping WOWs tied to learning remains at the forefront of their purpose. Yet a quality experience designed to *acknowledge* someone does wonders for self-esteem and confidence. An acknowledging WOW indirectly ties to learning. High self-esteem and confidence open up channels of learning. It allows for risk-taking, achieving, accepting challenges. WOWs that enter the school culture representing an effort to please, to provide useful tools to kick-start learning create an environment where learning can be fun.

Imagine the benefits of a safe learning environment filled with excitement and fun. So many students at younger and younger ages work at computers, search the Web, and hold technology in the palm of their hands 24/7. They have the world of fun and excitement to explore. It seems to me that we want to grasp that same energy and sense of exploration when they come to school to learn. Rather than have it be a downshifting of energy, using a WOW culture can uplift and allow that same energy to transfer transparently into the classroom.

Robert L. Fried in *The Game of School* says:

It's just that unless our children — of all ages — are truly engaged in their learning, most of what they experience during school hours passes over them like an undigested seed. They may be present in the classroom, but they are not really there. Their pencils may be chugging away on worksheets or the writing prompts or math problems laid out for them, but their intelligence is running on two cylinders at best.

(Fried, 2005)

It takes more than a simple WOW to engage all students to learn and run on more than two cylinders. But it's a darn good start and, used properly, can spell the difference between students going through the motions and those enthralled by learning.

Need for Novelty

WOWs bring novelty. From early on, the brains of Homo sapiens have been driven by the need for novelty, pleasure, and the avoidance of harm (Cloniger, 1987). Without these driving forces, we might never have left the cave!

In *Keep Your Brain Alive: 83 Neurobic Exercises to Help Prevent Memory Loss and Increase Mental Fitness*, authors Lawrence C. Katz, Ph.D. and Manning Rubin point out our brains need exercise and a break from routine. This is not to say the brain needs more of an activity, but rather needs a novel activity to break the passivity that occurs when the brain is not stimulated (1999).

Novelty allows for exploration, for discovery. It titillates us and makes us curious; lets us have fun. The more routines there are, the more options exist to pepper them with novelty. By their very nature, schools are predictable learning environments with a strong focus on rituals and procedures. This provides the perfect fodder for the creation of multiple experiences that are novel, exciting, curious, adventuresome, stress releasing, and fun. In short, WOWs.

Yes, too much novelty would create a chaotic situation. Yet too much routine breeds boredom, apathy, and downshifting of the brain too — often the default mode of many schools.

Are WOW experiences limited to students? Oh, no! We've already seen how teachers are acknowledged and tickled by a good WOW to start their year. And these can continue throughout the year. And spread to staff. And coaches and bus drivers and volunteers and office support. How about parents?

WOWs for Others

The Nail Bed

Principal Bruce Malnor at Ananda School in Nevada City, CA, doubles as a guinea pig. For parent night at the school, Malnor walks slowly across a stage to a square sheet of plywood lying on the floor. Hammered at every inch of the plywood are 16-penny nails. He gently lies on the nails while those attending look on astonished.

Next, one student puts an identical plywood board hammered with nails on top of Malnor, nails pointing toward him. On that board, the student lays a cinder block. Malnor lies very still, and another student with a sledgehammer comes up and smashes the hammer down onto the cinder block and the school principal!

Miraculously, Malnor survives! He stands up and takes a bow, and the parents applaud politely, most assuming it was a stunt. Just then, one of the students takes a bite out of an apple and slings it back over his shoulder and the apple lands on top of several nails. SPLAT! It breaks into many pieces. At that point, the response from the audience morphs from a WOW to a GASP!

Then the students commence to give their intended presentation on the laws of physics: inertia, force, pressure, dispersion of energy.

Pirates and Leaders

And how about using WOWs at conferences?

A National Educator Program Leadership Conference in Florida typically carries a theme for the conference. One year, half of a pirate ship was built to wrap around the main screen, which carried a continual display of PowerPoint® slides. There were masts on either side of the screen. The pirate ship helped people remember the pirate theme of "Discover the Treasures." It set the tone. It served as a peg from which they hung leadership qualities that tied to qualities one might find in a pirate. It sunk in. It got a WOW.

Speaking of pirates, the WOWs in this book actually occurred in various schools across the country. They can all be, um, "pirated" by anyone reading this book. That's what is called research!

It is perfectly all right to share WOWs. In fact, I encourage it. One WOW sparks an idea for another. At the beginning of the year, teachers can form groups and share lessons they will be covering. Then each group can share the most WOW lesson of the group. Or, develop a PowerPoint presentation to review district objectives and intersperse a WOW frame four or five times (the bright bold letters WOW! with sound). When that occurs, someone has to share a WOW with the group.

Sharing WOWs is another benefit of WOWs. You can be WOWed yourself, and then create one — or steal one — to share with someone else. As in the film *Pay It Forward*, where good deeds received had to be created for others, a good WOW deserves another. And another, and another, and another.

Shredding Your Fears

Remember the remedial reading teacher who held a funeral for "I can'ts?" I shared that video clip from *The Truth About Teachers* with staff at the University of South Florida's Suncoast Area Teacher Training (SCATT) while conducting a workshop on making quality instructional decisions.

Two of those participants, Freda Abercrombie and Dr. Jean Linder, head an intensive training program at SCATT for teachers wanting to achieve National Board Certification. To be a National Board Certified educator, participants must submit four portfolio entries, two of which include videotapes of themselves teaching an actual class along with a written, reflective critique of their teaching practices. They must demonstrate all professional teaching standards, complete tests on content knowledge across disciplines, and have taught a minimum of three years.

It's difficult! It's the equivalent to achieving a Master's Degree. And it's very public. Everyone knows the teacher is going for board certification — colleagues, students, family, and friends. If the teacher doesn't make it, everyone knows that too. Only an average of 44 percent of teachers make it on the first try.

Linder and Abercrombie coach these National Board candidates throughout their program. Yet they also recognize that, no matter how much coaching, there remains the fear factor. Some of these candidates are scared. There is fear in failure as well as success.

Keying off the idea of a funeral for "I can'ts," Linder and Abercrombie asked all the candidates to come to a conference room. They handed out several pieces of salmon-colored paper to each of the 40 or so gathered there. The candidates were asked to write down their fears on the paper — one fear per sheet of paper.

In the front of the room was a large, industrial-size shredder. When the candidates were finished, Linder and Abercrombie asked them to take their salmon-colored fears, form a line, and parade up to the shredder. As Linder and Abercrombie clapped and encouraged them, each candidate approached the shredder and "destroyed" their fears. Memorable WOW for them.

An indirect WOW for Linder and Abercrombie were the few candidates who showed real reluctance to shred their fears. They wanted to hold onto them a little longer!

More WOWs

Here are others off the top of my head.

A coach asks each member of his football team to pick a teacher to honor. Then at the home games, each teacher wears that player's away jersey all day and is introduced on the field at half time.

Students hold a prom night for teachers and their dates.

Create a WOW day where students WOW their favorite teachers. Or they create the WOW to begin a new lesson.

Develop a school-wide lesson where kids create a project about why WOWs work — brain-based research, testimonials, examples, and feedback.

Students make a pact that on a particular day when they ride the bus, they will: (a) be absolutely silent; or (b) sing a positive song in unison for the bus driver.

Schedule a parent night at a high school where students dress and act as their parents.

Quality, purpose, fun, novelty, and surprise = WOW.

We all deserve the wonder of a WOW.

What's yours?

Time to Share:
What Is in *Your* WOW Pocket?

We hope you are inspired to create a WOW experience or perhaps you have already. If you have a wonderful WOW you want to share, go to: www.plsweb.com/wow.

When you get there, you can send me an email explaining your WOW. Give me the gist of it along with your name and contact information. I will choose among those I receive to post on the site for others to read. And when we reprint this book, some WOWs you provide us will be used in the update — with your permission, of course. (You may also order more books at that site too.)

And if you enjoyed the book and don't have a WOW yet, I would love to hear your thoughts, comments, and ideas. Email me at: sbarkley@plsweb.com

References

Cloniger, R. (1987). *Brain/Mind Bulletin, 12,* 113. In Jensen, E. *Completing the puzzle* (p. 26).

Decker, B. (1992). *You have to be believed to be heard.* NY: St. Martin's Press.

Fried, R. L. (2005). *The game of school.* Somerset, NJ: John Wiley & Sons, Inc.

Glasser, W. (1992, May 13). Quality, trust, and redefining education, *Education Week,* 22-23.

Hart, L. A. (1998). *Human brain and human learning.* Updated. Kent, WA: Books for Educators, Inc.

Jensen, E. (1995). *The learning brain.* San Diego, CA: Turning Point Publishers.

Jensen, E. (1997). *Completing the puzzle: The brain-compatible approach to learning.* Del Mar, CA: The Brain Store.

Jensen, E. (1998). *Teaching with the brain in mind.* Alexandria, VA: ASCD.

Jensen, E. (2000). *Brain-based learning.* San Diego, CA: The Brain Store.

Katz, L. C. & Rubin, M. (1999). *Keep your brain alive: 83 neurobic exercises to help prevent memory loss and increase mental fitness.* NY: Workman Publishing Company, Inc.

Kovalik, S. (1993). *ITI: The model* (3rd ed.). Kent, WA: Books for Educators, Inc.

Madden, T. L. (2001). *Fire-up your learning.* Las Vegas, NV: Stratigent Press.

Maguire, J. (1990). *Care and feeding of the brain.* NY: Doubleday.

Meier, D. (2000). *The accelerated learning handbook.* New York: McGraw-Hill.

Peters, T. (1994). *The Pursuit of WOW!* NY: Vintage.

Rose, C. (1998). *Accelerated Learning for the 21st Century.* NY: Dell.

Scheibel, A. (1994, November). You can continuously improve your mind and your memory, *Bottom Line Personal, 15*(21), 9-10.

Scheibel, A. (1999, September). *Creativity and the brain.* PBS Teachersouce, Scienceline. ttp://www.pbs.org/teachersource/scienceline/archives/sept99/sept99.shtm

Sylwester, R. (1995). *A celebration of neurons: An educator's guide to the human brain.* Alexandria VA: ASCD.

The Truth About Teachers (1989). Hosted by Whoopi Goldberg. An Arnold Shapiro Production. Chatsworth, CA: AIMS Media.

Index

Note:

- Page numbers followed by n indicate footnotes.
- Page numbers followed by q indicate a quotation.
- Dashes followed by colons ("————:") represent the main heading in cross-references from one subheading to another.

A

Abercrombie, Freda: fear-shredding WOW, 65–67

Accelerated Learning, 18

    resources on, 17

Accelerated Learning school, 17

acknowledging (appreciative) WOWs, 60

Ananda School: nail-bed WOW, 63–64

Angert, Ruth: "We Didn't Start the Fire" WOW, 40–43

arousing curiosity: as the focus of WOWs, 6, 19–22, 25

attention-gaining. *See* arousing curiosity

autograph WOW, 43–44

B

balloon race WOW, 57–58

banana trick WOW, 54–55

body-mind events (movements), 17–18

    as state changes, 51–53

brain:

    the emotional brain and the intellectual brain, 32–33, 34

    novelty and, 17–18, 62–63

    state changes and, 51–53

brain research: and learning, 16

brain-based criteria for learning, xi, 17–18, 22

brain-based elements of WOWs, xi, 16, 18, 60

brain-compatible teaching and learning: resources on, 17

brass band WOWs, 30

briefcase-full-of-money WOW, 26–27

About the Author

Steve Barkley is a consultant and educator who serves as Executive Vice President of Performance Learning System, Inc. Steve has 27 years' experience teaching educators and administrators, working with school districts and state departments of education, as well as providing training in the private sector. He is a riveting and motivational keynote speaker, trainer, and consultant to educators and businesspeople alike.

Professional Development Opportunity

Steve Barkley is internationally recognized for his ability to facilitate change. His dynamic energy and focus provide a model for the skills necessary for effective change in schools and districts. For the past 30 years he has served as a consultant to school districts, teacher organizations, state departments of education and colleges. He has designed and conducted short and long term professional development training for both teachers and administrators. He also has extensive experience guiding districts through the process of school restructuring and site-based management.

Steve is a highly motivational and riveting speaker who is extraordinarily knowledgeable about life in the classroom. A catalyst for growth — he is a true role model who practices what he teaches.

If you would like to arrange a workshop, in-service training, keynote address, or consultation with Steve Barkley, contact:

Barry Zvolenski
Toll-Free: (888) 424-9700
bzvolenski@plsweb.com

For more information about Steve Barkley, go to
www.plsweb.com/sbarkley

PERFORMANCE
LEARNING SYSTEMS.